D0034707

51 CREATIVE IDEAS *for* MARRIAGE MENTORS

Resources by Les and Leslie Parrott

Books
51 Creative Ideas for Marriage Mentors
Becoming Soul Mates
The Complete Guide to Marriage Mentoring
Getting Ready for the Wedding
I Love You More (and workbooks)
Just the Two of Us
Love Is
The Love List
Love Talk (and workbooks)
The Marriage Mentor Training Manual for Husbands (for Wives)
Meditations on Proverbs for Couples
Pillow Talk
Questions Couples Ask
Relationships (and workbook)
Saving Your Marriage Before It Starts (and workbooks)
Saving Your Second Marriage Before It Starts (and workbooks)

Video Curriculum — ZondervanGroupware™
Complete Resource Kit for Marriage Mentoring
I Love You More
Love Talk
Mentoring Engaged and Newlywed Couples
Relationships
Saving Your Marriage Before It Starts

Audio Pages®
Love Talk
Relationships
Saving Your Marriage Before It Starts
Saving Your Second Marriage Before It Starts

Books by Les Parrott
The Control Freak
Helping Your Struggling Teenager
High Maintenance Relationships
The Life You Want Your Kids to Live
Seven Secrets of a Healthy Dating Relationship
Shoulda, Coulda, Woulda
Once Upon a Family
25 Ways to Win with People (coauthored with John Maxwell)
Love the Life You Live (coauthored with Neil Clark Warren)

Books by Leslie Parrott
If You Ever Needed Friends, It's Now
God Loves You Nose to Toes (children's book)
Marshmallow Clouds

Drs. Les & Leslie
Parrott

51 CREATIVE IDEAS *for* MARRIAGE MENTORS

CONNECTING COUPLES TO BUILD BETTER MARRIAGES

ZONDERVAN™

GRAND RAPIDS, MICHIGAN 49530 USA

ZONDERVAN.COM/
AUTHORTRACKER

ZONDERVAN™

51 Creative Ideas for Marriage Mentors
Copyright © 2006 by The Foundation for Healthy Relationships

Requests for information should be addressed to:
Zondervan, *Grand Rapids, Michigan 49530*

Library of Congress Cataloging-in-Publication Data

Parrott, Les.
 51 creative ideas for marriage mentors : connecting couples to build better marriages / Les and Leslie Parrott.
  p. cm.
 ISBN-13: 978-0-310-27047-8
 ISBN-10: 0-310-27047-2
 1. Church work with married people. 2. Mentoring in church work.
 3. Marriage—Religious aspects—Christianity. I. Parrott, Leslie L., 1964- II. Title.
 BV4012.27.P35 2006
 259'.14—dc22

2005031946

All Scripture quotations, unless otherwise indicated, are taken from the *Holy Bible: Today's New International Version®*. TNIV®. Copyright © 2001, 2005 by International Bible Society. Used by permission of Zondervan. All rights reserved.

The website addresses recommended throughout this book are offered as a resource to you. These websites are not intended in any way to be or imply an endorsement on the part of Zondervan, nor do we vouch for their content for the life of this book.

All rights reserved. No part of this publication may be reproduced, stored in a retrieval system, or transmitted in any form or by any means—electronic, mechanical, photocopy, recording, or any other—except for brief quotations in printed reviews, without the prior permission of the publisher.

Published in association with Yates & Yates, LLP, Attorneys and Counselors, Suite 1000, Literary Agent, Orange, CA.

Interior design by Beth Shagene

Printed in the United States of America

---

06 07 08 09 10 11 12 • 18 17 16 15 14 13 12 11 10 9 8 7 6 5 4 3 2 1

To Jason and Kelli Krafsky
and
Shane and Aimee Fookes
Two couples who share our passion
for awakening the sleeping giant.

CONTENTS

PART FOUR

IDEAS FOR MENTORING COUPLES IN DISTRESS

ACKNOWLEDGMENTS

Deep appreciation goes to our entire team at Zondervan — especially Paul Engle and Greg Clouse. Scott Bolinder caught the vision for awakening the sleeping giant the moment we mentioned it. This book never would have been written without the heartfelt encouragement and care of our Zondervan family. We can't say thanks enough.

We would be remiss if we did not also thank the many marriage mentors we have met across the country. You've been asking for a resource like this for years and we're so pleased to finally have it for you. Your passion for sounding the call to other like-minded couples who will join you in the cause of marriage mentoring is an inspiration, and we pray that this book will be another helpful tool in the important work you are doing.

Les and Leslie Parrott
Seattle, Washington

Let the wise listen and add to their learning,
and let the discerning get guidance.
PROVERBS 1:5

GETTING BIG RESULTS FROM THIS LITTLE BOOK

You wouldn't be reading these words if you weren't enthusiastic about helping other couples build better marriages. So right off the top, we want to say thank you. It's because of couples like you that countless marriages will be encouraged, strengthened, and even saved.

That's why we are excited to bring you this resource. For years, marriage mentor couples have asked for an "idea box" that would help them to be better mentors. We've heard questions such as:

"What can we do to help the newlywed couple we are mentoring to have better relationships with their in-laws?"

"We're racking our brains to find ways to help a mentoree couple move from a good marriage to a great marriage. Any suggestions?"

"Do you have any creative ideas that can help us get our 'couple in distress' to be more vulnerable?"

In our desire to assist, we would offer suggestions drawn from our own experience as mentors or from that of fellow mentors. Now, in this book, we're providing the first ever "idea box" for marriage mentors everywhere. And we're so glad you're looking into it.

We have worked with literally hundreds of mentor couples and have picked up many creative and clever ideas for making meaningful mentoring connections. Here we simply pass them on to you in hopes that your own wheels will start turning as you think of ways to mold the kind of relationship you desire and help your couple build a bond that lasts.

The Big Picture

This book is actually a follow-up to our larger volume, *The Complete Guide to Marriage Mentoring*. In it we explored exactly what a marriage mentor is and isn't. We talked about the common pitfalls that beginning marriage mentors make. We revealed the "boomerang effect" of marriage mentoring, the idea that mentoring other couples actually energizes one's own marriage relationship. But, perhaps most importantly, we devoted an entire section of that book to what we call the "marriage mentoring triad."

If this concept is new to you, of course, we'd suggest that you read *The Complete Guide to Marriage Mentoring*. But we can summarize here quite quickly and easily through this diagram:

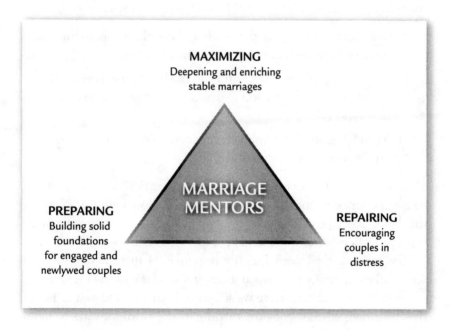

MAXIMIZING
Deepening and enriching
stable marriages

MARRIAGE MENTORS

PREPARING
Building solid
foundations
for engaged and
newlywed couples

REPAIRING
Encouraging
couples in
distress

As you can see, we propose that every marriage mentoring relationship fits within one of three areas: preparing, maximizing, or repairing. And chances are that you, as a marriage mentor, are inclined to do most of your mentoring with (1) engaged or newlywed couples, (2) couples moving from good to great, or (3) couples in distress.

It's for this reason that we have grouped the various creative ideas for marriage mentors into these three areas. Of course, many ideas work for mentorees across the board. That's why we begin with a section titled "Ideas for Mentoring Any Couple."

WHO THIS BOOK IS FOR

You are clearly interested in marriage mentoring. And if you are just curious to know what it's all about, we heartily invite you to read on. Or perhaps you are a seasoned and experienced marriage mentor couple looking for a few new tools for your marriage mentoring toolbox. This book is for you as well.

In fact, *51 Creative Ideas for Marriage Mentors* is written for all marriage mentors, regardless of age or stage. In *The Complete Guide to Marriage Mentoring*, we outlined the various levels of marriage mentoring positions common in a local church. Of course, there may be a pastor on staff who oversees this ministry. There's almost always a "point couple" who champions the cause of marriage mentoring in their congregation. We call them the "lead couple." Then there are typically three marriage mentoring "track couples," each dedicated to mentoring in one area of the marriage mentoring triad (preparing, maximizing, or repairing). And under each of these three marriage mentor couples, depending on the size of your church, there may be many other mentor couples as well as couples who facilitate small groups of couples. (See the diagram on page 16 for a visual representation of this structure.)

This book is for all of you—anyone and everyone who has anything to do with marriage mentoring.

Structuring a Marriage Mentoring Ministry

How to Implement the Marriage Mentoring Triad

Pastor

Pastor Recruitment
1. Present the marriage mentoring team model
2. Pastor to recruit marriage mentor lead couple
3. Marriage mentor lead couple to recruit
   three marriage mentor track leaders

Marriage Mentor Lead Couple

Marriage Mentor Lead Couple Responsibilities
1. Spiritual leadership of the marriage triad
2. Recruitment, training, and equipping of marriage mentors
3. Point of contact for funneling couples into triad categories
4. Hosting small group leader training
5. Coordinating marriage enrichment events (retreats, etc.)
6. Certified trainer of assessment tools

Marriage Mentor Track Leaders

"Preparing   "Maximizing   "Repairing
Track"   Track"   Track"

Marriage Mentor Track Leaders Responsibilities
1. Provide supervision of their respective triad track
2. Become certified in their triad track
3. Point of contact for couples seeking track training
4. Recruit small group leaders for track
5. Certified trainer of track assessment tools
6. Promote track throughout the church

Small Group Couple Responsibilities
1. Take part in small group leadership track training
2. Take the respective track assessment and expanded diagnostic
3. Recruit small group participants for their small group
4. Promote track throughout the church
5. Commit to replicate their group every 18 months
   (raising up a small group leader couple from their group)

Small Group Leaders

"Preparing Track"   "Maximizing Track"   "Repairing Track"
Small Group Leaders   Small Group Leaders   Small Group Leaders

GETTING THE MOST FROM THIS BOOK

Think of *51 Creative Ideas for Marriage Mentors* as a catalyst, not the definitive list of what marriage mentors can do to be effective, but a spark that will hopefully generate more ideas that aren't even included here. Or, you might find an idea in these pages and take it in an entirely different direction. That's great!

We aren't giving you a "to do" list for marriage mentors. These aren't actions you need to take, as if you were following a prescription. Instead, consider them a mechanism to help you more energetically approach your calling as a marriage mentor.

We also recommend that you thumb through this book and read just those portions that catch your eye. But don't feel compelled to read from beginning to end. Peruse it. Keep it handy. And then come back to it when you need a creative boost. Make notes in the margins. Fold down the corner of a page or mark it somehow to try later. In other words, make the book your own.

Sharing Your Ideas with Other Marriage Mentors

Invariably, as you are using this book, you will come up with a creative idea that works wonders for one of your mentoree couples. There are pages at the end of each section for you to record these ideas. But we'd love to hear about them too! In fact, thousands of other marriage mentors would love to hear about them as well.

That's why, on our website, in the extensive area devoted especially to marriage mentors you will find a place where you can share your creative ideas. So don't be shy. Let us all in on what's working for you. Simply go to www.RealRelationships.com and you'll see a place for doing just that. Of course, you will discover other creative ideas there from other marriage mentors. As we said, this book is simply a catalyst for what we hope will be dozens and dozens of ideas that become effective tools for marriage mentors everywhere.

We wish you every success as you bring some of the creative ideas in this book to your marriage mentoring relationships.

Les and Leslie Parrott
Seattle, Washington

PART ONE

IDEAS *for* MENTORING *Any* COUPLE

In this section you'll find several practical suggestions for mentoring any couple, no matter their age or stage. Feel free to make these ideas your own by changing them in ways that may work best with your mentorees.

CHAPTER 1

PRACTICE THE THIRTY-SECOND RULE

This little idea is a winner that works for every marriage mentoring relationship. And it's simple. Within the first thirty seconds of a meeting with your mentorees, say something encouraging to them. Give them an uplifting compliment.

This can be more challenging than you might think. Most of the time, upon meeting someone, we human beings focus on ourselves, searching for ways to make ourselves look good. Out of habit, we ask the generic "How are you doing?" Or, "Tell me about your day." That's fine, especially when it is genuinely focused on the mentoree couple, but if you truly want to see the spirits of your mentoree couple soar, try this thirty-second rule. Deposit good words in them before you even get started. Once you begin to practice this regularly, you'll see it really doesn't take all that much effort.

Everyone feels better when you give them attention and affirmation. So be sure to focus your attention, genuinely, on your mentorees right upfront. If you're distracted by something else at the beginning, that sets the tone for your time together.

Next, go out of your way to affirm them. Say something like, "You two always look so sharp," "I love the enthusiasm that exudes from you two," or "You guys have really been working hard, haven't you?" If nothing else, you can always affirm your mentorees for being mentored: "I'm so proud to be mentoring you two."

In thirty seconds' time, you just might say some of the most uplifting words they've heard all day.

CHAPTER 2

CURB MARRIAGE GOSSIP

Early on in any marriage mentoring relationship it is imperative to discuss confidentiality. Your mentorees will be put at ease if you assure them of your confidence. After all, they will only share information to the level that they know you are not going to be blabbing it to others — even strangers.

So take some time to explore this matter with them. Tell them flat out that the information that they share with you *stays* with you. Assure them that you would never betray their trust and that you will protect the information they share.

And while you're on the subject, you also might talk about "marital gossip." This is the all-too-common scenario that evolves when one spouse begins to talk to a friend or relative about their marital issues. Is this always inappropriate? Of course not. But it can soon become harmful if it makes the other spouse feel uncomfortable or embarrassed.

For example, if he doesn't want others to know he locked himself out of the car which in turn became the source of a marital spat, she should keep that information to herself. If she doesn't want others to know that she regularly loses her temper with the kids, he should keep that information to himself. But by expressing general frustration to a trusted, supportive friend in order to gain objectivity about a situation, they are not unduly embarrassing their partner nor are they complaining about specific behavior.

You get the idea. It basically comes down to helping them see the difference between seeking support from somebody outside the relationship versus venting feelings by complaining. And venting is almost always unhealthy for a marriage and damaging to a couple's sense of loyalty to each other. In fact, you can let mentorees know that if either of them wants to vent, you—as their marriage mentors—are a safe place for doing just that, as long as both spouses are present. (If you do this one-on-one, it creates an unhealthy triangle in your relationship with your mentoree couple.)

Here's a final thought that may help curb marital gossip. Have your mentorees consider the remarkable energy that would be restored to their marriage if they "gossiped" about good things instead of bad. If, for example, a wife confided in a friend how sweet her husband was to clean up the kitchen. Or if a husband told his friend how generous his wife was in giving to the needy. This is another way of saying that if you want to curb marital gossip, you can't go wrong by becoming your partner's publicist. In short, urge them to gab about the good with other people and never betray one another's confidence.

CHAPTER 3

PLACE A PHOTO OF YOUR MENTOREE COUPLE IN YOUR HOME

"In the very first session we had with our mentors," said one mentoree, "they asked us for a photo of the two of us. We gave them a five-by-seven portrait and the next time we were at their home I saw it framed and placed with some of their other photos. This really meant a lot to me. It made me feel like they really prized our relationship."

Of course, the real point of having a photo of your mentorees is not as much for them as it is for you. It's a tangible reminder of your role in their life, hopefully giving you pause to pray for them and be more conscious of their relationship each time you see it.

By the way, if they can't seem to find a photo for you, take one yourself. Some mentor couples report that this is standard practice at their first meeting.

CHAPTER 4

KEEP CONTACT INFORMATION HANDY

If you haven't discovered it already, you'll soon learn that one of the greatest hurdles to making a meaningful connection with mentorees is rarely the lack of good intentions. After all, like every other mentoring couple, you've volunteered for this experience. You want to be helpful. But if you are going to follow through successfully, you need to make it easy.

So, here's a simple suggestion that can't afford to go without saying: Keep your couple's names—along with their phone numbers, emails, and mailing address—posted in a convenient location. Place it near your phone in the kitchen or wherever you keep your personal contacts. That may be in an electronic address book or on your computer contact list.

When the information you need for contacting your mentorees is at your fingertips you are far more likely to drop something in the mail, send a quick email, or make a phone call.

CHAPTER 5

SEND A WORD
OF ENCOURAGEMENT

This may very well be the most simple suggestion we offer in this book — but it also affords some of the greatest impact on your mentorees. Every couple can be strengthened with a written note encouraging them in their marriage. Now, you may believe that a verbal compliment is enough. Sure, that's valuable. But research has revealed that when a word of encouragement is written down for another person, it is perceived as more genuine than when it is spoken.

Pastor and author David Jeremiah says, "Written encouragement comes directly from the heart, uninterrupted and uninhibited. That's why it's so powerful." We couldn't agree more. And by the way, we are talking about the old-fashioned way of sending an encouraging note. Consider this fact: Six days a week, regular mail service is provided by the United States Postal Service. Annually, postal workers handle 170 billion pieces of mail. Yet, in this huge sea of mail, officials say personal letters account for less than 4 percent of the total. So on average, the typical person will need to wade though twenty-five pieces of mail before putting his or her hands on one that contains a personal word. And more often than not, that personal word is not necessarily encouraging.

More than ever in this day and age, a handwritten note communicates that you care. So mail a note of encouragement to your mentoree couple from time to time. Even a brief card saying that you are thinking of them can be a real uplift.

CHAPTER 6

ASK THE ONE QUESTION THAT COULD CHANGE THEIR MARRIAGE

The best mentoring moments for couples come when the conversation engenders vulnerability and insight. It's the goal of every marriage mentor to bring about such moments in a conversation. Well, here's a way that nearly guarantees it, by way of a soul-searching question that's been proven effective time and again. You can use it whether you're mentoring newlyweds or a couple in distress. Are you ready? Here it is: *How would I like to be married to me?*

That simple question can do more to help your mentorees ensure the success of their marriage than almost anything else. Think about it. *How would I rate myself as a marriage partner? Am I easy to live with? How do I enrich the relationship? What are the positive qualities I bring to my marriage?*

If it fits your mentoring style and would meet the needs of your mentorees, you can even use this question as a way to introduce a few Scripture verses that describe qualities that make a person easy to live with.

For example, Paul wrote in 2 Corinthians 10:12: "We do not dare to classify or compare ourselves with some who commend themselves. When they measure themselves by themselves and compare themselves with themselves, they are not wise." Indeed, research has shown that partners who are easy to live with are not unduly concerned over the impression they make on others. They can throw back their head, breathe deep, and enjoy life—happy just to be themselves.

People who are easy to live with also have a way of passing over minor offenses and injustices. In other words, they are not easily offended (see Proverbs 17:9; 19:11).

People who are easy to live with are cooperative. They get along. They understand what the psalmist meant when he wrote, "How good and pleasant it is when God's people live together in unity!" (Psalm 133:1; see also Acts 4:32; Romans 14:19). They also have an even and stable emotional tone. Nobody is attracted to an uncontrollable temper (see James 1:19–20).

Healthy couples communicate their needs openly and honestly (see Ephesians 4:15). What they say is in sync with how they feel and what they want. They do not mask their feelings to protect their pride. Instead, they share their innermost thoughts, the good and the bad (see 1 Corinthians 13:6), even at the risk of occasionally hurting their spouse's feelings in the process.

Whether or not you use these Scriptures in your mentoring session, you can still ask this telling question. In fact, you can use it frequently by asking, "How would you have enjoyed being married to you this past week?" Explore what they think would have been good and what would have been challenging if they had spent the past seven days married to themselves.

CHAPTER 7

PASS ALONG A HELPFUL ARTICLE OR EMAIL

Do you read the newspaper? Magazines? Subscribe to an Internet news-letter? Or listen to a Podcast? Chances are that you come across an article from time to time that could be a real boost to the couple you are mentoring. It may not even be directly related to marriage, per se. You might read a business article on buying a first house. And maybe this relates to your couple. Or you may read an article on preparing "quick meals for two." Or maybe you come across an article on getting out of financial debt. You get the idea.

Of course, if you discover a piece on marriage that relates to something you recently discussed or would like to discuss together, this is a no-brainer. All it takes is a moment to clip out the article, attach a quick note, and send it off. Or if it's something you saw online or in an email, you might wish to forward it to them. Your mentorees will be thrilled to know you thought of them and that you are investing in their relationship in this way.

CHAPTER 8

TEACH THE SINGLE MOST POWERFUL MARRIAGE PRINCIPLE

The most shocking statement Jesus ever made about relationships holds enough power to revolutionize any marriage. He said: "If anyone forces you to go one mile, go with them two miles" (Matthew 5:41).

Every marriage mentor can help another couple to apply the "extra-mile principle" to their marriage Why? Because every husband and every wife knows how to walk the *first* mile. After all, our relationships couldn't survive without it. The first mile is what we know we have to do. It is taking out the trash, preparing dinner, or balancing the checkbook because we said we would do it.

So what's the second mile? The extra mile turns the ordinary into the extraordinary, the expected into the unexpected. We walk the extra mile for our partner, for example, when we take out the trash with a smile or prepare a meal with a special touch. The extra mile turns responsibility into opportunity. When we are walking the extra mile in marriage our attitude shifts from "have to" to "want to."

Common courtesy is an example of the extra mile in some marriages. Sounds funny, but courtesy isn't so common after being married to someone. We take "thank yous" and "your welcomes" for granted. We forget to say "please" at the table.

Here are some questions to help you explore this important principle with your mentorees:

- Do you want an "extra-mile marriage"? Are you willing to walk the extra mile for your spouse—even if your partner isn't?
- What is most likely to keep you from walking the extra mile in your marriage? Have weariness or busyness been obstacles for you?
- Do you think there's a price most couples pay for doing the bare minimum in their marriage? In other words, do "first-mile marriages" suffer from things that extra-mile marriages don't?
- Can you give an example of when you benefited from the extraordinary love of your partner, a time when he or she walked the extra mile for you?
- How can you work together to practice the extra-mile principle in your marriage? Consider some ways you might walk the extra mile for one another in the month ahead.

CHAPTER 9

LET THEM KNOW ABOUT A LOCAL MARRIAGE SEMINAR

Chances are that at some point during your mentoring experience you will learn that a marriage seminar or guest speaker on the topic is coming to your community. Whether sponsored by a local church or another organization, don't hesitate to make your mentorees aware of it. In fact, you may even want to attend the event together.

You may feel uneasy about suggesting a seminar that you don't know much about. That's okay. Let your couple know that. Say something like, "We heard about this marriage seminar coming to town and we don't really know anything about the speaker, but it might be interesting." And if they end up attending it and don't agree with various points the speaker made, this likely will generate some terrific talking points for your next mentoring session.

If your mentorees are reluctant to attend a seminar for any reason, don't push too hard. It's a fine line. You want to be encouraging, but not pushy. This is especially true when one of them (typically the husband) doesn't want to attend and the rest of you do. You don't want him to feel like you're ganging up to manipulate him into going. Still, it's worthwhile to explore any potential reservations for such an outing. And you can always give the reluctant spouse "veto power" once you're there—so that he (or she) has the power to say, "Let's do something else."

Some church libraries may have marriage seminars or workshops available on DVD. Watching a snippet of one of these together with your mentorees may be productive or a nice change of pace as well.

By the way, you can often track down your favorite marriage speakers' schedules by visiting their websites.

CHAPTER 10

BE AWARE OF "WHAT'S ON"

If you watch much television you'll undoubtedly come across a special news program, documentary, or other show that might have relevance to marriage and some of the issues you are exploring with your mentorees.

"Our mentors told us about a segment on *20/20* that related to in-laws," one couple told us, "and I'm so glad they did. It almost instantly changed the way we related to them." This may never have happened if their mentors hadn't alerted them. So keep an eye on the tube, if you are so inclined, and don't hesitate to keep your mentorees informed.

By the way, we know some mentors who will actually record relevant news segments to view together with their mentorees. Either way, be sure to debrief about the program when you can.

CHAPTER 11

OPEN THE CHURCH DOORS

Most of the time, you will have probably connected with your mentorees through your local church's marriage ministry. However, if you are mentoring a couple who is not attending a church, don't neglect to invite them to yours, but do so without applying pressure. If you come on too strong, they may see your mentoring as simply a ploy to get them to go to your church. Use discretion and approach this by putting yourself in their shoes. When an unchurched couple senses that you simply want them to experience something that's been great for your own relationship they will be much more open to it.

Much of our mentoring work with newlyweds occurs around our college campus, and many of these young couples haven't established a church life together. When we invite them to attend a church service or a program with us, they often feel honored — and many times begin to plug in to the church in meaningful ways.

CHAPTER 12

PRACTICE OLD-FASHIONED HOSPITALITY

"Can I take your order, please?" The scratchy voice comes from a small speaker just outside your driver's side window. You tell the lighted menu board what you want and then you "pull around to the pickup window" where your food, wrapped in colored paper and cardboard, is ready to go in a paper bag.

Sadly, too many meals these days begin this way. Enjoying a slow-paced, home-cooked meal around the dinner table has become a rarity, replaced by a fast-food pit stop. That's why it is especially meaningful when one couple invites another into their home for a meal. Plus, it's an excellent window into your own marriage for your mentorees to look through.

You've probably already thought of doing this with your couple, but we want to encourage you to actually extend the invitation. Don't get hung up on trying to be fancy or worrying about the menu. A simple spaghetti dinner is easy for most and always a hit. Or if you're not up for a home-cooked meal, just invite them for dessert.

We know some mentors who make an evening of it by having all the ingredients for a dinner that they make together with their mentorees. "We find that the shared activity of preparing a meal really relaxes our couples and makes conversations easier," said one experienced mentor.

Whatever your style, don't make excuses for a simple, home-cooked meal with your mentorees. Chances are that they will remember it for many, many years.

CHAPTER 13

BE ONE
OF THE FIRST
TO SEND A CHRISTMAS
GREETING

"Christmas," said Augusta Rundell, "is that magic blanket that wraps itself about us, that something so intangible that it is like a fragrance." And often the beginning of that intangible fragrance comes when we begin receiving Christmas cards. Remember this time-honored tradition when it comes to your mentorees. Be one of the first to send them a Christmas greeting. And be sure to include a personal message that lets your mentorees know that the greeting comes from your heart. Send them well wishes for a Christmas that brings their spirits together as they celebrate this sacred holiday. In other words, make the card about them (not just about you). You might even include a recipe for special Christmas cookies or something else that gives it a warm, personal touch.

CHAPTER 14

DOUBLE YOUR SERVE

Dietrich Bonhoeffer, the German theologian who was hanged by the Nazis during World War II, wrote a wonderful wedding sermon while he was in prison though he never had a chance to deliver it in person. The sermon included these words:

> Marriage is more than your love for each other. It has a higher dignity and power, for it is God's holy ordinance.... In your love you see only the heaven of your happiness, but in marriage you are placed at a post of responsibility toward the world and mankind. Your love is your own private possession, but marriage is something more than personal—it is a status, an office ... that joins you together in the sight of God.

Most couples have never thought about the "higher dignity and power" of their marriage. But it's a worthy topic of conversation for marriage mentoring. Why? Because we know of nothing else that can cultivate the intimacy of soul mates more than reaching out to the world as a team. Doing good for others as a couple brings a mystical quality into any marriage. It helps couples transcend themselves and become part of something larger.

Here's an idea that's not for everyone but one you may want to explore with your mentorees. What about the four of you doing something together for the good of others? There are literally hundreds of ways to incorporate shared service into marriage—offering hospitality in one of your homes (all four of you working together) to a group of single mothers on Mother's Day, volunteering at a homeless shelter, sponsoring a child in need, assisting in the church nursery, helping a shut-in to clean up her yard, or even going on a sponsored relief effort.

The apostle Paul says to "spur one another on toward love and good deeds" (Hebrews 10:24), and marriage mentoring can be a vehicle for doing just that. When we join our efforts in service together we are doubly blessed.

And whether or not you experiment with an act of service *with* your mentorees, you can still help them to explore how they can reach out in service as a couple on their own. The key is to help them find something that fits their personal style. One of the ways we enjoy reaching out as a couple is to do something anonymously. Even something small. We call it a mission of service in secret. It's an act of kindness concealed from everyone but the two of us. Our own sense of devotion and intimacy deepens as we secretly observe the results of our service together.

Two people joined in marriage, as Bonhoeffer said, are ordained to serve others as a team. As a partnership, two people can serve other people better than they could as separate individuals. So don't neglect the practice of shared service as you mentor your mentorees. It will do more to enrich the soul of their marriage than you might ever imagine.

Here's a line of questions to get the conversation going: *How can the two of you more effectively practice shared service in your marriage? What specific things might you do to reach out beyond the boundaries of your own marriage to meet the needs of others?*

CHAPTER 15

REMEMBER THEIR ANNIVERSARY

How many anniversary cards do you receive each year? Not many, right? But how thoughtful it is if someone remembers the day the two of you were married. Pass along this thoughtfulness to the couples you mentor by sending them an anniversary card or making an actual phone call with well wishes.

This is a special way of staying in touch with your mentorees—even after you are no longer in a formal mentoring relationship. We send anniversary cards to couples we haven't seen for quite some time. Why? It says something about your support of their marriage. Unlike a Christmas card that is sent with many others, an anniversary card takes more thought. You are singling out this couple by remembering the date they got married. And, make no mistake, they will take notice.

Why not mark your mentorees' anniversary on your calendar right now? In fact, you may want to make a note to yourselves several days in advance to mail the card so that it arrives on time.

YOUR ADDITIONAL IDEAS
FOR MENTORING ANY COUPLE

(Use the following pages to record any additional ideas
that you develop or come across and want to remember.)

PART TWO

IDEAS *for* MENTORING ENGAGED *and* NEWLYWED COUPLES

"Marriage is the fusion of two hearts," said Peter Marshall, "the union of two lives, the coming together of two tributaries." In this section we provide you with a few creative ideas on how you can be a better river guide as you work with a couple who is bringing two tributaries together.

Few adventures can compare to the thrill of starting a life together as husband and wife. As mentors, you can help your mentorees set a course for lifelong love.

CHAPTER 16

IDENTIFY THEIR TOP TEN NEEDS

If, early on in their relationship, newlyweds can identify and articulate the needs they are personally bringing into their marriage, they will be far more likely to get their needs met as well as meet the needs of their partner.

The following exercise will help your mentorees identify some of their deepest needs in a marriage relationship and communicate those to their partner. (The same exercise can be downloaded from our website, www.RealRelationships.com.)

Listed below are some of the most common needs that people identify as being important in marriage. Rate how important each of these items is for you. If you wish to add other items not included in our list, please do so. Do this on your own before discussing it with your partner and marriage mentors.

Need	Not That Important						Very Important
Admiration	1	2	3	4	5	6	7
Affection	1	2	3	4	5	6	7
Commitment	1	2	3	4	5	6	7
Conversation	1	2	3	4	5	6	7
Financial support	1	2	3	4	5	6	7
Honesty	1	2	3	4	5	6	7
Intimacy	1	2	3	4	5	6	7
Personal space	1	2	3	4	5	6	7
Respect	1	2	3	4	5	6	7
Shared activities	1	2	3	4	5	6	7
_____	1	2	3	4	5	6	7
_____	1	2	3	4	5	6	7

Now that you have completed your list, rank them in order of importance.

Order of Importance	Need
_____	Admiration
_____	Affection
_____	Commitment
_____	Conversation
_____	Financial support
_____	Honesty
_____	Intimacy
_____	Personal space
_____	Respect
_____	Shared activities
_____	_____
_____	_____

As marriage mentors, you can now help your newlyweds explore their lists in-depth. Have them reveal their results with you and their partner. What needs do both of them identify as important? As they discuss them, be sure they explain what each of their needs means to them. Men and women often mean different things even when using the same word (for example, intimacy). Finally, discuss how each of their needs might change as they grow in their marriage.

CHAPTER 17

HELP THEM SINK THEIR ROOTS DOWN DEEP

If the newlyweds you are mentoring are like most couples in America, they won't live in one place very long. In an average year, some forty million Americans move. Put another way, every ten years, between 40 and 60 percent of an average American town's population moves in or out. And get this. The average worker only keeps a job 3.6 years. So will your mentorees lengthen their roots and stay where you are for a good, long while? Probably not. If they are like most Americans they will move about fourteen times in their lifetimes.

Before our country was ribboned with interstate highways and before airplanes made cross-country travel easy, people stayed put much more than we do now. People had deep roots. These days one has to work pretty hard to lay down lifelong roots. It's not impossible, but it's rare.

However, there is a kind of rootedness in marriage that comes from being soul mates—and it's a point that will not be wasted on your mentorees. You may want to illustrate it to them this way: The root system of most trees is as wide and deep as the leaf line is wide and high. That is not true, however, of the redwood, which has a shallow root system that spreads out in all directions. That fact of life creates a problem for a redwood standing alone because it can be blown over easily due to its lack of stability. However when two redwoods grow together, their root structures intertwine and give one another strength. Though weak as separate trees, they become strong together.

The same is true for soul mates. "Two are better than one," said King Solomon.

Whether your mentorees live in one place for many years or relocate around the country according to job requirements, the most important roots they'll ever establish are in God and his Word. For this spiritual root system will bear much fruit. "I am the vine," said Jesus, "you are the branches. If you remain in me and I in you, you will bear much fruit; apart from me you can do nothing.... If you remain in me and my words remain in you, ask whatever you wish, and it will be done for you. This is to my Father's glory, that you bear much fruit, showing yourselves to be my disciples" (John 15:5, 7–8).

If you'd really like to drive home this point, you can do what some marriage mentors we know have done. Along with their mentorees, they have planted a couple of seedlings in the mentorees' yard or at an appropriate park to symbolize the rootedness of the newlyweds. As they grow, these trees can become a tangible reminder of this important lesson. For as a couple grows together in their understanding of God and his Word, they become all the more "rooted and established in love" (Ephesians 3:17). So if the life circumstances of your mentors take them from coast to coast or anywhere around the world, they'll never forget that soul mates, like the redwoods, become stronger together.

CHAPTER 18

CAUTIOUSLY CONNECT WITH YOUR MENTOREES' PARENTS

You'll definitely want to talk to your mentorees before doing this, but if they give you permission, it is a kind gesture (as well as informative) to connect with their parents. The sole goal is simply to say hello and to let these parents know how much you enjoy meeting with their kids in a mentoring relationship.

Typically, parents of engaged or newlywed couples are extremely grateful for this and will shower you with appreciation. Of course, if either set of parents is a little reserved, suspicious, or perhaps even a bit threatened, this will give you a significant window into a mentoree's family of origin.

One word of caution is in order. In some cases parents may attempt to "triangle" you into an unhealthy situation. For example, they may want to download a bunch of information you "need to know." Or they may want you to try to get their son or daughter to behave differently or ask you to pass messages to them.

If you sense any of this is happening, it's best to set boundaries. Be gentle but confident. Say something like, "I know you have great intentions, but it's probably best for you to have that conversation directly with your daughter (or son)." Among the reasons for setting these boundaries is that you will quickly lose the respect and trust of your mentorees if you don't. And, of course, you should never jeopardize your mentoring relationship by passing along information from them to their parents.

Keeping all this advice in mind, connecting with your mentorees' parents is a great idea if your mentorees are in favor of it. You can do this by phone, in person, or even with a kind email or note.

CHAPTER 19

DO SOME COUPON CUTTING

Even if it's been a while since you were newlyweds, you likely recall how newly married couples are often short on cash. And one way of helping them stretch their dollars is by giving them coupons for things they might use.

Simply clip coupons for various products over a few days and send them to your couple. If they tell you how they used them, you might continue this practice. If you get the sense that it's not really a big help to them, drop it.

"In our first year of marriage every penny mattered," said one mentoree. "And when our mentors gave us an envelope of coupons that they knew we'd use, it meant a lot to us."

The key here is to give deliberate coupons, not just a bunch of random ones you happen to get in the mail yourself. If you know they will use a pizza coupon or a discount on specific grocery items, those are the coupons to pass along.

By the way, many people find it helpful to search for coupons online. In fact, the websites dedicated to coupon cutting are too many to list. A simple search of "coupons" will render plenty of options to consider.

CHAPTER 20

CONSIDER A BABYSITTING OPPORTUNITY

Most newlyweds eventually talk about starting a family and they often idealize and romanticize the whole experience of parenthood. Of course, becoming parents *is* a wonderful experience, but it's not always what they expect. So it can be particularly helpful—even long before a couple starts a family—for them to get a taste of parenting by babysitting together.

If you have children at home, or have friends who do, you might consider having your mentorees "try on parenting" by spending an evening alone with the children or even by staying with them while you have a weekend away.

Of course, this would need to be a scenario that your mentorees are motivated to experience and that comes naturally out of the relationship you have with them. You certainly don't want to give the impression that you want them to serve you as child-care workers.

If your mentorees do end up babysitting, be sure to debrief with them, not only to find out about how the kids did, but what it was like for them as a couple. Ask them what they learned about themselves in the experience: *What kind of parents do you think you'll be? How do you think you will differ from each other in your parenting style?*

CHAPTER 21

GIVE THE IN-LAW INVENTORY

Because the issue of in-laws is so critical to this stage of marriage, you may want to bring the issue up explicitly—even if your mentorees don't. A starting point may be to reminisce about how you and your partner experienced in-law situations during your first year. Also try an open-ended question about how each of your mentorees is feeling about relating to both families.

The following inventory may be yet another way to generate a more open discussion on the topic. Read aloud the beginning of each statement to your mentorees and have them choose the sentence completion option that fits best. Let them know that there are no right or wrong responses.

In relating to my in-laws I:

☐ feel very comfortable in knowing what to call them.

☐ wish I knew what to call them (Mom, Dad, or first name).

I feel that my spouse is:

☐ too close to his/her family.

☐ not close enough to his/her family.

My spouse feels that I am:

☐ too close to my family.

☐ not close enough to my family.

I wish:

☐ I felt more comfortable with my spouse's family.

☐ my spouse felt more comfortable with my family.

My spouse and I disagree over:

☐ how much time to spend with family.

☐ whose family to visit for the holidays.

I sometimes feel pulled between:

☐ what my family wants from me and what my spouse wants from me.

☐ my loyalty to my own family and my loyalty to my spouse's family.

Since our wedding, my relationship with my own family:

☐ has changed for the better.

☐ has changed for the worse.

Since our wedding, my relationship with my spouse's family:

☐ has changed for the better.

☐ has changed for the worse.

Now use their answers as a springboard for airing some of their feelings and ideas about in-laws.

CHAPTER 22

MAKE A SPLASH
WITH A LOW-COST GIFT

Newlyweds, of course, have typically been showered with gifts—the pun is intentional. As marriage mentors, you certainly don't need to feel compelled to add to their bounty. However, sometimes a big impression of how much you care can be made with very few dollars.

One marriage mentor couple we know likes to give a "cookie kit" to their mentorees and bake cookies while they are meeting together. Here's their system: They shop discount stores for an inexpensive cookie sheet, mixing bowl, spatula, timer, a couple of cookie cutters, and potholders, and then gather it all in an inexpensive basket along with a favorite cookie recipe. They also purchase the actual recipe ingredients, include those in the basket as well, and tie it with a bow.

They tell us that with some of their couples it becomes a tradition to bake cookies at each of their meetings, using a new recipe each time. In fact, they joke that they often can recall a particular conversation by connecting it to the cookies they made that evening. "It was the night we made peanut butter cookies and talked about money management." You get the idea.

CHAPTER 23

CHART THEIR SPIRITUAL JOURNEY

Everyone has a unique spiritual pilgrimage. Yet many newlyweds never really delve deeply into understanding their new spouse's journey. As marriage mentors you can help them better understand the spiritual paths they are joining together.

Begin by talking about the value of merging their two journeys. Assure them that this does not mean giving up their individuality or uniqueness but joining their spirits as they learn to walk together with God.

Here are a couple of exercises that you can use to get your mentorees thinking about this important truth. Both are available in a downloadable format at www.RealRelationships.com.

> You may have grown up in a religious home learning Bible verses, going to Sunday school, and studying at a religious college. Or maybe you never went to church while growing up and are just becoming grounded in faith. Whatever your story, take a moment to gather your thoughts about your own spiritual quest. Make a few notes in the box on the next page of some of the significant mile markers that would describe your journey.

Next, have the couple take a minute or two to complete this brief questionnaire:

Agree	Disagree	Spouses should ...
☐	☐	pray together every day.
☐	☐	study the Bible together regularly.
☐	☐	discuss spiritual issues.
☐	☐	go to the same church.
☐	☐	agree on theology.
☐	☐	pay tithe.
☐	☐	pray for each other.
☐	☐	leave each other's spiritual life up to God.
☐	☐	have the same level of spiritual maturity.
☐	☐	attend church at least once a week.

Once the mentorees have finished both exercises, have them share their journey with each other as you facilitate the discussion.

CHAPTER 24

MAKE THEIR FIRST NOEL ONE TO REMEMBER

If you'd like to be kind to your budget, this idea requires some advance planning—perhaps even before you know the couple you'll be mentoring. How does it work? Well, post-Christmas sales offer a great opportunity to pick up holiday items at very low prices. And one marriage mentor couple we know takes full advantage of this by creating a "First Christmas Together" box for the newlyweds they mentor.

They simply fill an inexpensive plastic tub (with a lid for easy storage) with a variety of tree ornaments, strings of lights, personalized stockings, holiday books, and other decorative items. They also include a warm greeting, reminding the newlyweds of "the reason for the season," and when they present the gift (typically after Thanksgiving) they talk about the value and importance of celebrating Christmas as a couple and establishing new holiday traditions that are uniquely their own.

CHAPTER 25

EXPLORE THEIR ROLES

Why is it important for your newly married mentorees to bring their unconscious marital roles into awareness? Because the more aware they are of their roles—as a husband and a wife—the more likely they are to enjoy a satisfying relationship.

Ask mentorees to complete the following sentence stems on their own (you can download a form to facilitate this at www.Real Relationships.com). Have them write whatever pops into their head as they complete the sentences. Generally their first thought is the most important.

Husbands are ...

Wives are ...

Marriage is ...

Next repeat the exercise, having each of them write down how their mother would complete the same three sentences. Finally, repeat it once more, having them write down how their father would complete the sentences.

Now help them compare their sentences with each other and discuss their responses. Ask them to compare how either one of them would be like their same-sex parent and how their expectations about their spouse's role might be influenced by the home they grew up in. In most marriages, a close correlation exists between parents and partners, and with few exceptions the traits that match up most closely are the negative traits. Have your mentorees make a conscious effort to decide what roles each will play.

CHAPTER 26

NOTE THE LITTLE THINGS

The honeymoon is supposed to be, as *Merriam-Webster's Collegiate Dictionary* says, "a period of unusual harmony following the establishment of a new relationship." And it often is. Why? Because newlyweds have been particularly intentional about how they treat each other during these romantic days they've dedicated to their love.

What most newlywed couples can't seem to see is that the honeymoon will soon be over. It's inevitable. Of course, they want to believe that their entire marriage will be one long honeymoon. But eventually, real life sets in. There are bills to be paid, errands to be run, problems to be solved, and so on.

How does all this impact your mentoring of newlyweds? Because you have an opportunity to help them make something they instinctively do on their honeymoon a lifelong habit. We sometimes call it the honeymoon habit. And it has to do with "the little things."

Indulge us with a silly illustration: Have you ever been bitten by an elephant? Probably not. Have you ever been bitten by a mosquito? Of course. Like we said, it's a silly illustration, but it makes a point: Little things often matter most. Especially in marriage. Too often, we think on a grand scale about romance — creating the perfect once-a-year getaway — and neglect the little opportunities that present themselves every day in marriage.

You will be doing your mentorees a huge favor if you can get them to continue focusing on the little things they do to make their relationship more loving.

For example, have them consider how they greet one another when returning home from work. If they begin by making a consistent effort to reconnect with a tender touch or embrace at the end of their day, they will establish one of the most important patterns couples can have for setting a positive tone for their evening together.

"Well, of course we'll do that," they may tell you. That's when you may want to respond that the vast majority of couples end up with what researchers call the "grocery list" connection: *Did you pick up my dry cleaning? I'll need the car tomorrow. What's for dinner?*

But if they start with a tender touch before they get to the nitty-gritty tasks of the day, they will create an aura of love in their home that leads to a level of fulfillment most married couples only dream about. Sure, it's a little thing, but it makes a huge difference when it becomes a habit.

Have them come up with other "little things" to develop a honeymoon habit. Be sure they don't forget saying "please" and "thank you," given the fact that politeness is one of the first things to go in a new marriage. In some ways this reflects increasing levels of comfort, but left unchecked, it can lead to rudeness. One researcher revealed that when paired with a stranger, even many newlyweds were more polite to him or her than they were toward each other. But if they establish a pattern of politeness now, they'll likely be even more polite on their fiftieth wedding anniversary!

CHAPTER 27

ENVISION THEIR GOLDEN ANNIVERSARY

What will your marriage look like in fifty years?

This is a question most newlyweds never consider. But if they did, it just might help them chart their course to that golden anniversary with a lot more intention. So why not pose the question to your mentorees?

What will you reminisce about on your fiftieth wedding anniversary? Can you picture your future together? Encourage them to be specific. Where will they live and what will they be doing? What kinds of memories will they treasure most?

We know some mentors who give their mentorees a special remembrance after a session involving this question. It's nothing fancy, maybe just a personal card with a verse inscribed in it. Perhaps Proverbs 23:18: "There is surely a future hope for you, and your hope will not be cut off." Or Proverbs 24:3–4: "By wisdom a house is built, and through understanding it is established; through knowledge its rooms are filled with rare and beautiful treasures."

After fifty years, what memorable treasures will your mentorees' house of love include?

YOUR ADDITIONAL IDEAS FOR MENTORING ENGAGED AND NEWLYWED COUPLES

(Use the following pages to record any additional ideas
that you develop or come across and want to remember.)

PART THREE

IDEAS *for* MENTORING COUPLES *Moving from* GOOD TO GREAT

"There is no more lovely, friendly, and charming relationship," said Martin Luther, "than a good marriage." We couldn't agree more. But we'd be quick to add that there is also no more amazing, breathtaking, and enriching relationship than a *great* marriage.

In this section you will find several creative ideas for helping a good couple enjoy greatness as husband and wife. How do we define a "great marriage"? There's no hard and fast definition, but you might think of "great" couples as those whose relationship is in the top 10 percent of all married couples. These are couples who are not perfect, just deeply content and happy. They make each other better people. They draw one another closer to God. These marriages represent what every couple longs to enjoy.

CHAPTER 28

DREAM BIG

One of the great starting places in mentoring a couple from good to great is to get them dreaming. What do they want from their life together? Business consultants working with companies call it a BHAG — a "big, hairy, audacious goal."

What's your couple's BHAG? When your couple dreams unfettered about their future, what do they see? Where would they like to be one year from now? Five years? Ten years? Twenty-five years?

We have a plaque in our home with the following inscription from Henry David Thoreau: "If one advances confidently in the direction of his dreams, and endeavors to live the life which he has imagined, he will meet with a success unexpected in common hours." It reminds us to talk about our dreams.

What we consciously dream about, what we envision for our future together, the goals we set for our partnership determine the quality of our marriage in the present. For, to paraphrase Proverbs 29:18, "Where there is no vision, a marriage will perish." But if our dreams are worthy and filled with godly hope they take us to heights we never imagined.

Of course, it is possible to have dreams that are not godly. So how should a Christian couple dream, according to the Bible? Consider this paraphrase of Paul's words in Philippians 4:8: "Whatever is true, whatever is noble, whatever is right, whatever is pure, whatever is lovely, whatever is admirable — dream on those things." The focus of a healthy dream and vision is not on "laying up treasures on earth," but on pleasing God.

Help your mentorees to dream. And dream big! It was H. W. K. Moule who rightly said, "The frontiers of the kingdom of God were never advanced by men and women of caution."

CHAPTER 29

FIND INSPIRATION AROUND YOU

One of the defining qualities of a couple in the top 10 percent of all married couples is their knack to be inspired—by each other, by creation, by nearly anything. This exercise will help you mentor your couple toward doing just that.

Few things will join a couple's spirits like a moment that inspires both husband and wife. Begin your session by having them each recount a few of these moments from their own life (whether they shared them together or not).

For instance, ask questions such as:

- What happens within you personally when you are inspired by something you've read, heard, or seen? Do you have a physiological response? Are you more motivated? What about your emotions? Consider these questions and complete this sentence: *I know I've been inspired when ...*
- Next, note the last time you were truly inspired. How long ago was it? What inspired you? Did you share it with anyone?
- Note two or three of the most inspirational moments of your entire life and why they stand out to you (it may have been a speech or sermon you've heard, books you've read, movies you've seen, people you've met, an event you attended, etc.).

Now have your mentorees consider how they can bring more inspirational moments into their marriage by answering the following questions together as a couple:

- What kinds of places are we most likely to encounter inspirational moments (e.g., a site with historical significance, our church, hiking in the wilderness)?
- Where are we as a couple likely to encounter people who might inspire us (e.g., a volunteer agency, a children's center)?
- What things can we do together that would heighten our inspiration quotient (e.g., rent movies of motivational stories, read a biography of a couple who overcame something that seemed insurmountable)?
- What couples can we socialize with who would likely bring more inspirational moments into our marriage (e.g., a couple at church who has a story to tell)?

Inspirational moments cannot be coerced or conjured up at will. They are discovered. Spontaneously. But we can avail our spirits of the places, people, and experiences where they are more likely to occur.

If this exercise is particularly helpful to your mentorees, consider having an "inspiration check-in" during each of your sessions to help them become more intentional about noting moments of inspiration they share.

CHAPTER 30

TURN THE TABLES

Have you ever stopped to ask someone for directions? You roll down your car window and quiz a passerby, "Can you tell me if there's a pharmacy around here?" Almost always, people stop whatever they're doing and help if they can—even if it means crossing the street or standing in traffic. They may even repeat the directions a couple of times to make sure you understand. Why? Because whenever people feel they know something that you don't, it gives them an ego boost. It all stems from the universal need to be needed.

That's why this little idea can be so powerful. Here's how it works. After you have established a good relationship with your mentorees (sometime beyond the first few meetings), ask them for advice when a topic comes up about which the two of you would especially like to learn more. You'll be amazed at how they come alive.

"You know, tonight I'd like to turn things around a little bit here," you might say. "We've been having this little battle all week—it's nothing big—but I thought you two could help us." You'll have their undivided attention at this point. "We are feeling very differently about how to spend a block of free time we have coming up." Describe the situation a bit and then ask, "So what would you do if you were in our shoes?"

Of course, you don't want to do this with an issue that is truly volatile or heavy. It's not your mentorees' role to get involved with you in that way. Choose a nonthreatening topic, one that will simply give them an opportunity to help you out. Their input and advice also will provide you a window into how they approach certain situations, which you might broach later in your mentoring discussions. For now, you simply want to listen, interact, and, above all, show appreciation. By the way, the next time you meet, it's also a tremendous compliment to again underscore how much they helped you.

CHAPTER 31

MORE TIME
OR MORE MONEY?

A key insight for mentorees moving from good to great can come when you pose this simple question: *Would you rather have more money or more time?* The question is sure to generate an interesting discussion. Consider how you personally would you answer it.

A little fewer than half of those polled a number of years ago would take the cash.[1] Indeed, assuming that survey is still accurate, 51 percent of us would rather have more free time even if it means less money; although according to another survey, 35 percent of us would rather earn more money even if it means less free time. The rest of us can't quite make up our minds![2]

The connection between time and money has always been tight, especially for those in the fast lane. When *Fast Company* magazine asked its readers about the connection, they phrased it this way: If you could have one more hour per day at home or a $10,000 a year raise, which would you choose?

How would your mentorees answer? Would they rather have an extra hour at home each day or the extra dollars? If they chose the money, they're among the majority of *Fast Company* readers. A whopping 83 percent of them said money, while only 17 percent said they'd take the extra time at home.[3] This may say more about *Fast Company* readers than it does about the general population, given the fact that reams of research over the years have confirmed most often people would take time over money.

Either way, this simple question will help your mentorees clarify their values and work toward what matters most to them at this stage of their marriage.

CHAPTER 32

THE MOST INFLUENTIAL PERSON

This little exercise will give you an insight into what your mentorees want most in their marriage. Have them each write down (without sharing their thoughts) the name of the one person outside their immediate family who has had the greatest positive impact and influence on them. Next, have them write down who they think their spouse will write down.

They may need a moment to think about this. Once they have recorded their particular person's name, have them share it and explain why they selected that person. Then have the other spouse reveal who they thought their spouse would choose. Give them time to explain their predictions as well.

Next, have them discuss the influence these two individuals have had on their marriage—whether it was directly or not.

Finally, challenge your mentorees to write a note to their influential individuals (assuming the person is still living) expressing their heartfelt appreciation of how they impacted them individually as well as their marriage. Why? Because expressing gratitude always moves a person from good to great.

CHAPTER 33

HOMEWARD BOUND

One of the most productive times a husband or wife can have toward the end of their workday (or whenever they've been apart for at least several hours) is to take three or four minutes along their route home to visualize their spouse. Have them imagine what their spouse's day was like and how he or she might be feeling. Encourage them to think about what they might say to their partner upon entering the house.

Why is this valuable? Because it gives your mentorees a structured way to be intentional about their marriage. And being intentional is what makes the difference between a good marriage and a great one.

CHAPTER 34

"I LOVE YOU MORE THAN ..."

One of the defining characteristics of a couple in the upper 10 percent is how they express their love for each other. They don't settle for the reflexive "I love you." Instead, they make sure the message sinks in.

How? By comparing their love to something they know will be meaningful to their spouse. You see, comparisons establish value. If you know a particular car you've never heard of is comparable to a Mercedes, you have a good idea of its value.

The same is true when a husband or wife compares their love for their partner to something important or valuable by completing the simple sentence stem: "I love you more than. . . ." Challenge your mentorees, for the next week, to think of comparisons they can make to express how much they love their spouse.

They can choose activities, foods, and experiences that their spouse will find pleasurable and dear to their heart. Here are two examples from our friend Paul Lewis: If you are a golfer, you might declare, "I love you more than a hole in one!" If your favorite travel destination is Hawaii, you might say, "I love you more than a perfect Maui sunset." You get the idea.

Once each of your mentorees has formed seven comparisons, have them keep them on hand for a good moment to deliver one per day in the coming week. They may write it on a card, whisper in their spouse's ear, say it just before falling asleep, at the opening or close of a phone call, or after asking: "Do you know how much I love you?"

While this may not be an idea that works for every couple, for some it just may become an anticipated daily habit.

CHAPTER 35

DECISIONS, DECISIONS!

Every couple who is moving from good to great learns to work as a team—especially when it comes to making decisions. After all, experts estimate that about 25 percent of every couple's conversations involve that very thing.

Take time to explore decision-making with your mentorees. Begin by asking them to recall the three most important decisions they've made as a couple in the past year or two and the process that went into making those decisions. What worked well for them and what didn't?

Next, have them note the three most important decisions they have made as a couple this past week. Again, what helped them get to a consensus?

The goal of this exercise is to help them identify their decision-making style as a couple—and to help them hone areas of decision-making where they could improve. You can be sure that the next decision they make, they will be more cognizant of the process. In fact, you may want to bring up this issue again at your next mentoring session and review any decisions they've recently made and how they may have done things differently.

CHAPTER 36

MONKEY SEE, MONKEY DO

Every competent parent knows that the most important wedding present they will ever give their children is the gift of their own healthy relationship. Why? Because kids carry into their own marriage much of what they saw practiced by their mom and dad.

This exercise helps your mentorees take a good look at what "lessons" they are teaching their kids about marriage—whether they know it or not. It begins by having your mentorees consider what, in specific terms, their children (no matter their ages) would know about marriage if all they had done was observe their parents' relationship over the past month. This can be a daunting task for mentorees. Help them to be honest and specific.

Next, have them consider what they would have preferred their children learn about marriage from them over the past month. What can they do to ensure that this will be the marriage lesson they teach in the month ahead?

CHAPTER 37

START A DATE CLUB

Ask almost any healthy, growing couple about their schedule and eventually they will tell you about "their night." Whether it's once a week or once a month, successful couples build a "date night" into their schedule—even if they have kids. Strike that. *Especially* if they have kids.

If your mentorees are struggling to make this a reality ("babysitters are too expensive"), here's a suggestion that works wonders. It's called a "date club" and it guarantees them three dates a month with free babysitting! All your mentorees need to do is find three other couples who will agree to reserve one Saturday night a month in rotation to serve as the sitters for the children of the other three couples. On the other three Saturdays of the month, each couple has time for an evening out.

Don't force this idea on your mentorees or make them feel guilty if it doesn't fit their style. But if you encounter reluctance, you might suggest that they try a trial period, say three months.

Let's get specific on what needs to take place. They need to recruit three other couples who: (1) have children similar in ages to their own, (2) have a compatible parenting style, and (3) live close enough to keep drop-off and pick-up times short. They also will need to agree on a few guidelines, including mealtime arrangements for the kids and date "curfew." And, of course, there needs to be such flexibility in the date club that everyone will understand when plans must change due to illness or emergency.

Finally, make sure your mentorees guard against using their Saturday night date club for purposes other than enhancing their marriage. This is not a time to run errands or clean the house. The purpose is to enjoy each other and build a better marriage.

CHAPTER 38

PAY NOW, PLAY LATER

Delayed gratification. The very words cause some to get the jitters. Why? Because the ability to patiently put off immediate rewards in order to enjoy greater benefits later goes contrary to our nature. Nevertheless, it is another defining quality of couples who live life well.

Saving money is a prime example. Think of the pain and heartache that could be avoided by countless couples if only they would practice a little more delayed gratification when it comes to their spending habits.

But delayed gratification does not just apply to saving money. It is a principle that applies to all of living. Acclaimed student of human behavior Scott Peck once wrote: "Delaying gratification is a process of scheduling the pain and pleasure of life in such way as to enhance the pleasure by meeting and experiencing the pain first and getting it over with. It is the only decent way to live."[4] Scheduling the easy and the hard applies to everything from cleaning the house to earning an education.

For this reason, as you mentor a couple from good to great you really can't afford to skip this particular topic of conversation. They need you to help them explore their ability to delay gratification.

One of the things they need to know is that the key to delayed gratification is patience. It's a virtue endorsed time and again in Scripture. Patience, for example, is a fruit of the Spirit (see Galatians 5:22). As Paul prayed for Christians, he often asked God to give them patience (see Colossians 1:11). And the book of Hebrews characterizes the Christian life as an exercise in patience (see 6:12; 12:1 – 3).

Putting our immediate gratification temporarily in abeyance can strengthen the marriage bond. Couples who do not develop the capacity for delayed gratification become impulsive and are soon swayed by every whim of the moment. But couples who forgo some instant pleasures cultivate discipline and reap meaningful and fulfilling rewards. "Patience," as a German proverb says, "is a bitter plant but it bears sweet fruit."

Here are some questions to help you explore the topic of delayed gratification with your mentorees:

- How do each of you practice the art of delaying gratification? Does it come easier to one of you than it does the other?
- Give an example of how you personally have patiently practiced delayed gratification.
- Name one or two areas in your lives that could benefit from the discipline of delayed gratification. How could you as a couple practice it?
- How could practicing delayed gratification buoy your marriage?

CHAPTER 39

THE BIG QUESTION

One terrific exercise your mentorees can do on a weekly basis is simply to ask their spouse "The Big Question." Here it is: *What could I do today or tomorrow that would make me a better husband or wife?* It takes no more than ten minutes and to ensure the best results, here are the steps the couple should follow:

1. Ask your partner if he or she is willing to answer "The Big Question": What could I do today or tomorrow that would make me a better husband or wife?
2. If he or she agrees, prepare your mind to be objective and open to giving as well as receiving personal information. Lower your guard and warm your heart.
3. On scratch paper, note one thing your spouse could do right now to be a better marriage partner to you.
4. On that same paper, note one thing that already makes your spouse a good marriage partner. Be sure you have in mind an example from the past week that backs up your point and makes it concrete.
5. Once you have both made your notes of one good thing and one area for improvement, take turns sharing your thoughts.
6. Finally, don't nag your spouse about how he or she could improve — make your suggestion during this exercise and then leave it there, until the next time you do "The Big Question."

Again, this is an exercise that can become a weekly habit for your mentorees — as well as for you.

YOUR ADDITIONAL IDEAS
FOR MENTORING COUPLES MOVING
FROM GOOD TO GREAT

(Use the following pages to record any additional ideas
that you develop or come across and want to remember.)

PART FOUR

IDEAS *for* MENTORING COUPLES *in* DISTRESS

Whether the result of a bad decision or bad circumstances, a couple in distress needs help. And as a mentor to these couples you are in a powerful position to do something very special for them. That's why we devote this section to providing you with several creative ideas that will lift the spirits of a hurting couple.

Langdon Mitchell said, "Marriage is three parts love and seven parts forgiveness." He may be right, but for a couple in distress there may be several other important ingredients to making their marriage what it once was or what they long for it to be. And one of those things is having more fun. So you'll find a few ideas on doing just that as well as other ideas that are more penetrating and poignant.

CHAPTER 40

TAKE INVENTORY

The following exercise adapted from our *I Love You More Workbook* is one we've found to be particularly helpful at the beginning stages of mentoring a couple in distress (download a copy for each spouse from our website, www.RealRelationships.com). It's a way of taking inventory of anything that may be threatening your mentorees' marriage. Every couple has their own unique list, but here are some of the most common threats (mentorees should check all that apply):

- ☐ Frequent conflict
- ☐ Financial pressures
- ☐ Power struggles
- ☐ Busy schedules
- ☐ Work pressures
- ☐ Career crisis
- ☐ Infertility
- ☐ Tumultuous relations with extended family
- ☐ Rebellious child
- ☐ Sexual unfulfillment
- ☐ Lack of spiritual intimacy
- ☐ Frequent communication breakdowns
- ☐ Major illness
- ☐ Addictions
- ☐ Infidelities and lack of trust
- ☐ Grief or loss
- ☐ Other: _____

The exercise continues as each spouse takes a few more minutes to note at least a half dozen things that are good for their marriage right now. Their list could consist of anything from "having a date night each week" to "being honest with each other" to "sharing the housework"—whatever buoys or strengthens their marriage in spite of bad things. Here's the list we provide them to get them thinking:

- [ ] Being honest with each other
- [ ] Sharing housework
- [ ] Shared humor or laughter
- [ ] Having strong social support
- [ ] Sharing a vision for our future
- [ ] Enjoying a committed church life together
- [ ] Fulfilling sex life
- [ ] Having a date night
- [ ] Blessing of having good children
- [ ] Physical health
- [ ] Secure financial future
- [ ] Shared interests and hobbies
- [ ] Strong extended family relationships
- [ ] Supporting each other in prayer
- [ ] Secure in our marriage commitment
- [ ] Emotional health
- [ ] Other: _____

Once your mentorees have made their two lists, ask them to share this information with each other in your presence. Your job is to keep this time from becoming a gripe session. The goal of sharing their first list is simply to identify the difficulties they are both contending with that impact their marriage, while sharing the second list is to help them focus on the good, not just the bad.

Doing this exercise with your mentorees early on will help you quickly understand exactly why they need you as their mentors.

CHAPTER 41

STEER CLEAR
OF THE NUMBER-ONE
MARRIAGE PROBLEM

"You're not listening to me!"

We hear this statement more than any other when mentoring couples in distress. No surprise. The number-one marriage problem reported by couples in general is a breakdown of communication.

A sage once said that the Lord gave us two ears and one mouth, and that ratio ought to tell us something. Good point. We often think of good communication skills as learning to express ourselves more clearly, getting our message across. However, 98 percent of good communication is listening.

The word *listen* occurs more than three hundred times in the Bible. The book of Proverbs says, "To answer before listening—that is folly and shame" (18:13). And the book of James reminds, "Everyone should be quick to listen, slow to speak and slow to become angry" (1:19).

What do your mentorees need to know about listening? Basically one thing. Listening is not passive. It is not sitting back, quietly hearing what their partner has to say, waiting for their turn to talk. Listening is active, getting involved with their partner's message to accurately understand it. The point of active listening is nothing more than letting their partner know that they are in tune with him or her. A good listener doesn't give advice or try to solve problems. A good listener listens.

How can you help your mentorees become better listeners? By helping them practice. Consider doing a couple of role plays—just the two of you—in front of your mentorees. Demonstrate to them what active listening looks like. There's no need to make this elaborate. Just a minute or two of talking about a real-life issue is all that's required.

Next, have your mentorees talk about something that often becomes heated between them. They can do this in front of you as you coach them to actively listen to each other. Focus on encouraging them. Point out ways they listen well and when you see an area where they could do better, say so gently. You definitely don't want to be preachy.

Another good set of questions to pose is: *When do you most often want to be listened to by your partner? How do you convey this to him or her? Or do you?*

You may want to ask your mentorees to provide an example of how they each benefited from a recent communication with one another—a time when their spouse was an especially good listener. This may prompt a bit of self-examination, often revealing just how much they need to practice this skill.

CHAPTER 42

TURN MURPHY'S LAW ON ITS EAR

Attitude. It can make a world of difference in how two people view the same thing, especially in marriage. What one of us sees as troubling, the other may see as exciting—the only difference is attitude. And few things are more toxic to a couple than a bad attitude that pervades a good marriage. For this reason we feel it's imperative to explore the attitudes of every mentoree couple in distress.

"The longer I live the more I realize the impact of attitude on life," writes Chuck Swindoll. "Attitude, to me, is more important than facts. It is more important than the past, than education, than money, than circumstances, than failures, than successes, than what other people think or say or do. It is more important than appearance, giftedness, or skill."

Swindoll goes on to say that the most remarkable thing about life is that we can choose our attitude every day of the year. "We cannot change our past. Nor can we change the fact that people will act in a certain way. We also cannot change the inevitable. The only thing we can do is play on the one string we have, and that is our attitude."[5]

If you want to know the makings of a miserable marriage, Murphy's Law sums it up succinctly: "Nothing is as easy as it looks; everything takes longer than you expect; and if anything can go wrong, it will and at the worst possible moment."

Positive couples live by another law: "Nothing is as hard as it looks; everything is more rewarding than you expect; and if anything can go right, it will and at the best possible moment."

Do an attitude check with your mentorees. Have them rate where they fall, as individuals, on the continuum of these two laws. Then ask them to talk about their rating—for in the very process of doing so they are more likely to cultivate a positive outlook.

Be prepared, however, for the naysayer mentoree who may argue that having a positive attitude in his marriage is "overly optimistic." Hear him out. Don't argue. In fact, agree with him. It *is* overly optimistic, but a good attitude is exactly what opens the double doors of marriage for optimism to do its work. Optimism, you see, creates opportunities and solutions we normally don't notice. Without optimism, couples see no way out of their negative circumstances. *My spouse will never change*, they say. *We've tried everything and it doesn't help.* Without optimism, even good couples consider their situations as hopeless and eventually give up.

CHAPTER 43

WHAT WOULD YOU MISS?

"Did you miss me?" Every spouse utters this question at some point after being away from their partner for a while. After all, we all want to know that our presence makes a difference. When we're not around we want to know that our spouse noticed. In fact, we want to know that they were eager to have us back, right?

Well, here's a sobering exercise that is often an eye-opener even for couples in distress. Begin a discussion with your mentorees by exploring the fact that life's routines always seem to lull us into believing today's relationships will be around tomorrow. It would be unhealthy to constantly worry that this isn't true, but it is equally important to remember that bad things happen to good people. It seems that individuals who have unexpectedly lost a loved one, or who thought they were going to die and didn't, always seem to say that the experience created a permanent reminder to value life today. Ask your mentorees if they've ever experienced this in their own relationships (with other family members, friends, and so on).

Next, take it to a more personal level and have them answer this question: *What if your spouse were suddenly gone from your life?* As we said, this is a sobering exercise but it may be just what the doctor ordered for your couple.

Have your mentorees focus their thoughts not on some tragic scenario that might have created this unexpected departure or death, but rather on what they would miss most if their spouse were permanently gone. It might be the other person's thoughts, emotions, laughter, security, spirituality, homemaking, parenting, whatever.

If you feel it would be helpful, the two of you may share your own answers to this question. Remember, vulnerability by a mentor couple (when appropriate) begets vulnerability from mentorees.

The bottom line of this exercise is that it often makes the most distressed couples more grateful for their spouse than they ever imagined. Like the popular song says, "You never know what you've got 'til it's gone."

CHAPTER 44

REVEAL THE TWO MOST OVERLOOKED "ROMANTIC" PHRASES

When mentoring couples in distress it is often helpful to get back to the basics. That's why it can prove powerful to remind them of two little statements that work wonders for couples encountering tough times.

Here they are:

"I was wrong."

"Will you forgive me?"

Our friend Paul Lewis calls these phrases the most overlooked "romantic" words ever spoken by couples. And we tend to agree. Why? Because they engender humility. And humility is essential to overcoming marital mountains.

So ask your mentorees how often they utter these phrases and what difference it makes when they do. Be sure to have them focus on themselves—not each other. This is not a set-up for blaming each other for not being more humble!

CHAPTER 45

GIVE THEM A REPUTATION TO UPHOLD

Here's an idea that has more to do with how you think about your mentorees than what you say or do with them.

Dr. J. Sterling Livingston, formerly of the Harvard Business School, observed, "People perform as consistently as they perceive you expect them to perform." We agree. Especially when it comes to mentoring. When you are mentoring a couple in distress they will often perform at the level you expect. If you believe they won't exert any effort to change their spending habits or to manage their emotions, for example, you'll probably be right. But if you have confidence in your mentorees' capacity to curb their spending and get out of debt, or to control angry outbursts, you somehow instill their ability to do just that.

A reputation is something that many people spend their entire lives trying to live down or live up to. So why not help your mentorees by giving them a positive reputation to uphold? Of course, this can go beyond just holding your beliefs to yourself. Let them know you have confidence in them. Say things like, "We believe this is the week when you two are going to really see a difference in your marriage because you're focusing on empathy." Or, "We're predicting that by the next time we see you two that you'll have several stories to tell of how you avoided what would normally have been big conflicts."

To paraphrase German philosopher Johann Goethe, "Treat your marriage mentor couple as if they already were what they potentially can be, and you will make them what they should be."

CHAPTER 46

THE COUPLES-COMMUNICATION STRENGTHS FINDER

While it's tempting to focus solely on a distressed couple's deficits, much can be gained by helping them focus on what they do well. The following exercise is a tool for helping your mentorees articulate their couple-communication strengths. Because communication impacts everything in marriage, no matter a couple's particular struggle (see our book *Love Talk*), if they can begin to recognize ways they communicate well it will give them courage and hope to overcome their hurdles. (You can download the questionnaire, one for each partner, at www.RealRelationships.com.)

It is the rare couple that periodically articulates what they do well as a team. Think about it. Most couples are more prone to complain about their pitfalls than they are to praise themselves for their successes. If we aren't careful, there's something about the nature of relationships that causes us to exchange pep rallies for gripe sessions. Don't fall into this temptation — especially as it relates to your ability to communicate.

Begin this exercise by scanning the list below and marking things you do well and things your partner does well. Once you have done that, review your column of check marks and note which items you both do well and which items neither of you do particularly well. Feel free to add to this list any communication abilities that are missing for you. And, as always, the more honest you are, the more helpful this exercise will be to you.

Who does this well ...	You	Spouse	Both	Neither
Listening without interruption	☐	☐	☐	☐
Staying on topic	☐	☐	☐	☐
Being ready to apologize	☐	☐	☐	☐
Controlling emotions appropriately	☐	☐	☐	☐
Giving full attention	☐	☐	☐	☐
Identifying and expressing feelings	☐	☐	☐	☐
Thinking clearly before speaking	☐	☐	☐	☐
Reserving opinion until the right time	☐	☐	☐	☐
Maintaining eye contact while talking	☐	☐	☐	☐
Being appropriately vulnerable	☐	☐	☐	☐
Permitting productive conflict	☐	☐	☐	☐
Speaking with clarity	☐	☐	☐	☐
Inviting and receiving feedback	☐	☐	☐	☐
Appropriately using humor	☐	☐	☐	☐
Coming across as personally warm	☐	☐	☐	☐
Expressing more genuine interest	☐	☐	☐	☐
Being assertive with needs	☐	☐	☐	☐
Knowing when to talk and when to not	☐	☐	☐	☐
_____	☐	☐	☐	☐
_____	☐	☐	☐	☐

The items that you checked "both" are what you perceive as your current couple-communication strengths. Those which you think neither of you do particularly well are your current couple-communication deficits.

Now, compare notes with each other as your mentors facilitate a conversation to help you see which items you *both* agree are your current communication strengths. If you don't have any at this point, relax. Things can change. And if you have several, good for you!

As mentors, remind your couple that their strengths will change. These aren't set in stone. And likewise encourage them that they will get better at other aspects of communication—and you are going to help them do just that.

CHAPTER 47

EXPLORE THE LESSON OF AN OLD FARM COUPLE

Looking for a way to help your mentorees enjoy more encouragement from each other? Take a lesson from an old farm couple who learned how to signal each other when they needed extra encouragement.

If the husband needed a little emotional boost, he'd walk into the kitchen and throw his hat down on the table. That was his signal to his wife that he could use a little more encouragement from her. When she saw his hat on the table she would say something like: "I know you've been working hard today and I really appreciate you mending that clothesline for me."

Similarly, if he discovered that his wife was wearing her yellow apron, it was a signal that he needed to comfort her with a few encouraging words. He'd then say something like: "You must be exhausted after your busy day. Have I told you lately how much I love you and appreciate what you do for me?"

Makes sense, doesn't it? Of course, such behavior could border on insincerity if one partner doesn't take it seriously or if one of them abuses the signal by using it too often. But it's worth a try. Why not help your mentorees establish some specific signals for encouragement? Think of the difference it might make in their marriage.

Of course, the best way to teach this skill is to model it. In other words, practice this strategy in your own marriage and you'll be able to show your mentorees just how it works. Then, explore some potential options of what encouragement signals they might use in their marriage relationship. It might be lighting a candle. It could be using a specific tablecloth or place mats. You get the idea. Any tangible signal that is easily identifiable will work. The point is to foster more encouragement when it is needed.

CHAPTER 48

AVOID THE BLAME GAME

Have you noticed that everyone seems to be a victim? The media has. *The New Yorker* magazine, for example, recently featured a cover story with the title "The New Culture of Victimization" and the headline of the inside story was "Don't Blame Me!" On the cover of a recent *Time* magazine these words appeared: "Cry Babies and Eternal Victims!" *Esquire* followed with an article titled "A Confederacy of Complainers." It seems people these days don't want to be held accountable.

We will leave it to the social commentators to explain just how our new culture of victimization will affect us long-term, but we know exactly how it can affect a marriage. Once a husband or wife gets wrapped up in the blame game (blaming parents, genes, a boss, each other), a vicious cycle of shirked responsibility permeates the relationship. Soon each partner is looking for ways to avoid responsibility and shift the blame. Of course, this is nothing new. Ever since Adam blamed Eve, and Eve blamed the serpent, we have learned the trick of finding excuses. Accused of wrongdoing, we respond, "Who me?" "I didn't do it," "It's only a game," "Well, you asked for it," or "I didn't mean to."

And chances are that the distressed couple you are mentoring has fallen into this tempting blame game. What can you do? Bring it to their attention. Start with a nonthreatening question or two such as: *Have you noticed society's temptation to be a victim? Why do you think so many people are quick to blame others (like the lawsuit against a fast-food chain for making a customer fat)?*

You might then focus on the positive by asking them to give you an example of a time when they decided to rise above their negative circumstances by taking responsibility (and not blaming others). Ask: *How did you adjust to something that was beyond your control? How does your spouse demonstrate personal responsibility? What mature choices have you seen him or her make?*

Finally, explore this question with them: *In practical terms, what can you and your partner do to foster a blame-free relationship?*

Remind your couple that life is a series of personal choices. Once they realize this, they become free (see Galatians 5:13) — free to take responsibility for their feelings and actions, even when circumstances aren't what they hoped for.

CHAPTER 49

SHOULDA, COULDA, WOULDA

Marriage offers many opportunities for partners to feel guilty. In a survey assessing "Who makes you feel most guilty?" the majority of respondents confessed they were the key perpetrators of their own guilt. But next on the list was "my spouse."

Research has revealed that much of the guilt we experience is undeserved. It is false guilt, and causes us to suffer self-punishment needlessly. Our internal tape recorder says: "You should *always* have the house clean," "You should *never* come home late," or "You should *never* make a mistake."

Guilt is certainly a topic that deserves attention when mentoring couples in distress—especially if one of the spouses suffers from low self-esteem. Merely talking about guilt is enough to alleviate some of the heavy burden, but there also are practical things you can do with your mentorees to battle its harmful influence.

First, make it clear that each of us is born with an inner judge and jury. We are in the courtroom daily, waiting to hear the verdict: guilty or not guilty. Not that the decision has any bearing on the truth. It is our emotions, as much as reality, that will determine the verdict. For at the root of self-imposed guilt is the idea that what we feel must be true—in other words, if we *feel* guilty, we think we *must* have done something wrong. However, emotions can lie, because they are not products of reality, but of our *interpretation* of reality. The psalmist alludes to this when he says, "Troubles without number surround me; my sins have overtaken me, and I cannot see" (Psalm 40:12).

Feelings of guilt cause blurry vision. That's why it is important for your mentorees to learn to give one another grace. They need to help each other see reality as it is, so that they can avoid needless self-punishment.

Following are what we have found to be productive conversation starters on this subject:

- Some Christians believe God wants them to feel guilty. Do you have a hard time believing that there is "no condemnation for those who are in Christ Jesus"?
- Give an example of a time in your life when you were afforded grace instead of guilt. What did that do for you?
- Discuss the difference between true guilt and false guilt and how both affect marriage.
- When are you most tempted to make your mate feel guilty? Why?
- What are some real-life situations where you might give one another more grace?

Of course, the saddest form of false guilt comes in not believing in and accepting God's grace and forgiveness. As the apostle Paul writes: "Therefore, there is now no condemnation for those who are in Christ Jesus, because through Christ Jesus the law of the Spirit who gives life has set you free from the law of sin and death" (Romans 8:1–2).

As you explore the subject of guilt with your mentorees, realize that this may become an opportunity to provide healing in their relationship. So prepare yourself for this session by praying about it beforehand.

CHAPTER 50

WHAT'S YOUR FAVORITE?

Most couples in distress are so focused on their problems that they rarely put energy into any lighthearted aspect of their relationship. Here's what you can do to help them change that.

Casually ask them to tell you about their favorite restaurant. A nonthreatening question like this will typically engender a fond memory. Take a moment to enjoy that memory with them.

Next, ask them if they've ever made a list of "couple favorites." You can be assured that they haven't. Help them construct such a list by considering several things they favor most as a couple. If they can't agree on a favorite in a particular category, keep moving. Here are a few categories to consider:

What's their favorite ...

- Board game
- Television show
- Joke
- Grocery store
- Pastime
- Song
- Gift to give
- Sport
- Relative
- Christmas tradition
- Movie
- Homemade dessert
- Automobile

- Vacation destination
- Coffee shop

Add others to the list as appropriate. The goal is to help your mentorees focus on things they share together. When a couple begins to talk about their favorites they become a "we" rather than two "I"s.

CHAPTER 51

WHAT HAVE YOU BEEN LOOKING FOR?

Everyone is looking for something—especially in marriage. We call it a couple's marriage mind-set. Helping a couple in distress understand their marriage mind-set is one of the most important things you can do for them. Why? Because their mind-set, after all, has nothing to do with anyone but them, as a husband and wife. This exercise will help each of them become aware of what they are looking for in each other. And it will help them see how that impacts their marriage. (You can download this exercise, one copy for each mentoree, from our website, www.RealRelationships.com.)

You view your marriage partner through a series of filters. Below is a list of these filters. Look through it and check the six or so most descriptive of how you view your partner.

☐ Accepting	☐ Careless	☐ Demanding
☐ Adaptable	☐ Caring	☐ Dependable
☐ Aggressive	☐ Cheerful	☐ Dependent
☐ Annoying	☐ Clever	☐ Determined
☐ Anxious	☐ Cold	☐ Disciplined
☐ Bitter	☐ Confident	☐ Efficient
☐ Brave	☐ Conforming	☐ Elusive
☐ Calm	☐ Controlling	☐ Energetic
☐ Carefree	☐ Critical	☐ Friendly

- [ ] Gentle
- [ ] Giving
- [ ] Greedy
- [ ] Gruff
- [ ] Gullible
- [ ] Helpful
- [ ] Helpless
- [ ] Idealistic
- [ ] Inconsiderate
- [ ] Innovative
- [ ] Insensitive
- [ ] Intelligent
- [ ] Irresponsible
- [ ] Irritable
- [ ] Jealous
- [ ] Kind
- [ ] Lazy
- [ ] Manipulative

- [ ] Naïve
- [ ] Narcissistic
- [ ] Negative
- [ ] Noisy
- [ ] Objective
- [ ] Oblivious
- [ ] Passive
- [ ] Patient
- [ ] Perfectionistic
- [ ] Petty
- [ ] Playful
- [ ] Principled
- [ ] Protective
- [ ] Rational
- [ ] Reactionary
- [ ] Reasonable
- [ ] Reassuring
- [ ] Regretful

- [ ] Relaxed
- [ ] Reliable
- [ ] Respectful
- [ ] Rigid
- [ ] Self-conscious
- [ ] Self-righteous
- [ ] Spontaneous
- [ ] Stubborn
- [ ] Tactful
- [ ] Tender
- [ ] Trusting
- [ ] Trustworthy
- [ ] Understanding
- [ ] Unpredictable
- [ ] Visionary
- [ ] Witty
- [ ] Worried

Once you have checked the top half-dozen ways you tend to view your spouse, determine whether they are mostly positive or negative (the list is composed of forty filters in each category). In the space below, note the negative filters through which you tend to view your spouse and when you are most likely to use them.

Filter: _____. I see this quality when my spouse . . .

Filter: _____. I see this quality when my spouse . . .

Filter: _____. I see this quality when my spouse . . .

Filter: _____. I see this quality when my spouse . . .

Once each of your mentorees has completed this exercise, help them consider ways that they might counter their negative filters with a more positive mind-set. For example, ask: *What are ways you could view this specific negative behavior more positively?* With an open mind, this discussion can be a turning point in changing their mind-set, not to mention their marriage, for the better.

YOUR ADDITIONAL IDEAS FOR MENTORING COUPLES IN DISTRESS

(Use the following pages to record any additional ideas
that you develop or come across and want to remember.)

WHERE DO WE GO FROM HERE?

We again want to remind you that this compilation of ideas for marriage mentors is just a jumping-off place. Be sure to make them your own. Change them in ways that will work best for you.

And please don't forget to share your own creative ideas for marriage mentoring. You'll find a forum for doing just that at www.Real Relationships.com. Besides, you'll want to check out what other mentors are contributing to the mix. The ideas for becoming more effective marriage mentors are infinite and we will continue to bring you the very best of them at the website.

We began this book by thanking you for your efforts as a marriage mentor couple. And we want to say it again. It's because of couples like you that countless marriages will be encouraged, strengthened, and saved.

We wish you every success in your marriage mentoring endeavors.

NOTES

1. B. Kanner, *Ladies Home Journal* (October 1, 1998).
2. *U.S. News & World Report* (December 11, 1995).
3. *Fast Company* (July/August 1999), 112.
4. M. Scott Peck, *The Road Less Traveled* (New York: Simon and Schuster, 1978), 18.
5. Charles Swindoll, *Improving Your Serve* (Waco, Tex.: Word, 1981), n.p.

For All Your Marriage Mentoring Needs Log on to www.RealRelationships.com!

Log onto www.RealRelationships.com to join the Parrotts' Marriage Mentor Club. For a limited time you can become a charter member for FREE!

Here's just some of what you will find there:

- Downloadable tips, forms, and helps

- On-line training modules

- Mentor and mentoree evaluation tools

- Forums, chat events, and other means of interacting with mentoring experts and other mentors like you

Drs. Les and Leslie Parrott are internationally known, bestselling authors. They have been featured on *Oprah*, *CBS This Morning*, CNN, and *The View*, and in *USA Today* and the *New York Times*. They are also frequent guest speakers and have written for a variety of magazines. The Parrotts serve as marriage ambassadors for the Oklahoma governor's ten-year Marriage Initiative.

www.RealRelationships.com

PREPARE

Saving Your Marriage Before It Starts: Seven Questions to Ask Before (and After) You Marry

Drs. Les and Leslie Parrott

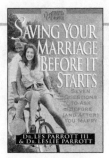

Do you long for real, honest advice from a couple who knows the hopes and struggles of today's couples? Do you want to build a marriage that will last a lifetime? *Saving Your Marriage Before It Starts* shows engaged couples and newlyweds how they can identify and overcome stumbling blocks to a healthy marriage.

Marriage Kit: 0-310-20451-8	Hardcover: 0-310-49240-8
Workbook for Men: 0-310-48731-5	Workbook for Women: 0-310-48741-2

MAXIMIZE

Love Talk:
Speak Each Other's Language
Like You Never Have Before

Drs. Les and Leslie Parrott

Couples consistently name "improved communication" as the greatest need in their relationships. *Love Talk* is a deep yet simple plan full of new insights that will revolutionize communication in love relationships.

Hardcover: 0-310-24596-6   DVD: 0-310-26467-7
Workbook for Men: 0-310-26216-7   Workbook for Women: 0-310-26213-5

REPAIR

I Love You More: How Everyday
Problems Can Strengthen Your
Marriage

Drs. Les and Leslie Parrott

I Love You More explores how a marriage survives and thrives when a couple learns to use problems to boost their love life, to literally love each other more.

Softcover: 0-310-25738-7   DVD: 0-310-26582-7
Workbook for Men: 0-310-26275-5   Workbook for Women: 0-310-26276-3

Interested in hosting the Parrotts for one of their highly acclaimed seminars? It's easy. Just visit www.RealRelationships. com to learn more and complete a speaking request form.

Les and Leslie speak to thousands in dozens of cities annually. They are entertaining, thought-provoking, and immeasurably practical. One minute you'll be laughing and the next you'll sit still in silence as they open your eyes to how you can make your relationship all it's meant to be.

"I've personally benefited from the Parrotts' seminar. You can't afford to miss it."

GARY SMALLEY

"Les and Leslie's seminars can make the difference between you having winning relationships and disagreeable ones."

ZIG ZIGLAR

"The Parrotts will revolutionize your relationships."

JOSH MCDOWELL

"Without a doubt, Les and Leslie are the best at what they do and they will help you become a success where it counts most."

JOHN C. MAXWELL

Learn more about the Parrotts' "Becoming Soul Mates Seminar" and their new "Love Talk Seminar."

*Click on www.RealRelationships.com
to bring them to your community.*

We want to hear from you. Please send your comments about this
book to us in care of zreview@zondervan.com. Thank you.

GRAND RAPIDS, MICHIGAN 49530 USA

ZONDERVAN.COM/
AUTHORTRACKER